Free & Opensource Video Editor Software
For Windows, Ubuntu Linux & Macintosh

by

Cyber Jannah Studio

2018

Prolog

The complete list free and opensource video editor software available on Windows, Ubuntu Linux, BSD & Macintosh for college student, youtube creator and indie movie maker.

La lista completa de software de edición de videos libre y de código abierto disponible en Windows, Ubuntu Linux, BSD y Macintosh para estudiantes universitarios, creadores de youtube y productores independientes de películas.

Free & Opensource Video Editor Software

1. Avidemux Video Editor

AviDemux is an application whose aim is to help you encode and edit video files easily. A small tool, AviDemux will do its job fast and it is perfect for adjusting home-made videos. Use it for MPEG, AVI, DivX, VCD, SVCD and DVD MPG and you won't need other complex software.

AviDemux's GUI is dedicated to the average user and it has an intuitive, user-friendly interface.

In a basic window you will be introduced to various processing tools, decoder options, filters and frame rate configurations.

Subsequently, you can edit, cut, append and filter videos and re-encode them to AVI or to MPEG 1/2. This virtual item is similar to VirtualDub, but the difference is that you can encode VCD/SVCD/DVD mpg too.

AviDemux supports the most common codecs (M-JPEG, MPEG, DivX, Xvid, huffyuv, WMA and so on) since it is fitted with libavcodec and libmpeg2. The application also offers support for audio formats like MP3, WAV and OGG.

The latest versions of AviDemux come with advanced features aimed at the various types of operations you may perform, regarding image export, audio, editor, TS/Demux, MP4/Demux and subtitle capabilities.

The developers of this application have managed to ensure proper initialization of Qz for jpeg export, fixed importing MP2 audio detected as MP3, fixed deleting chunks of the video leading to seek errors, better detection of double PFS input files, better TS/Demux initialization (avoiding dropping audio), fixed issue when source has more than 4 tracks, fixed management of PCM audio and many others.

AviDemux is the proof that you can encode and edit video files even if you are not an expert and that a simple piece of software can attract stellar user reviews and be reliable as well.

You don't necessarily have to learn how to use a complex software in order to get professional results.

Link Download http://avidemux.sourceforge.net/

2. Shorcut Video Editor

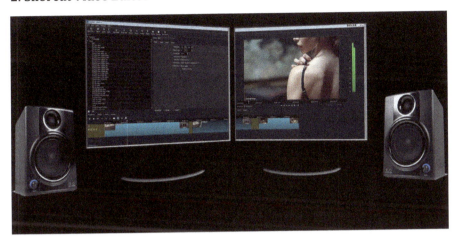

Shotcut is a powerful video editor allowing you to get the most from your favorite videos, from converting them to other formats to applying filters and merging files.

Shotcut relies on FFmpeg to support a wide range of audio and video formats and easily switch between them: VOB, MXF, M4A, FLV, M2T, MP4, AVI, MOV, MPG, OGG, MOV, WEBM and so on.

The software also provides support for image formats like BMP, JPEG, GIF, PNG, TGA, SVG, TIFF, and SVG.

Shotcut works with the MLT XML format as well – you can open these files as clips, perform tests, create playlists, encode them and stream them to a network of your choice.

Aside from working with a diversity of formats, Shotcut uses a multi-format timeline, which means you can mix videos having different resolutions and framerates.

You can create a whole new aspect of your videos by applying a variety of video filters, such as Crop, Glow, Blur, Mirror, Saturation, Sharpen, and so on. For color correction and grading use "Color Wheels". Audio filters include Balance, Gain and Pan and help you easily solve audio file issues.

Other features you may find useful are screen and webcam capture, audio capture, network stream playback, the recent files panel, the drag and drop functionality, batch processing, and support for 4K resolutions.

Shotcut's complexity lies in both its advanced editing options, like 3-point editing, and in its interface options (you can choose between native OS look and custom dark and light).

Shotcut provides a very wide range of editing options for a free app; you'll need some time to uncover all its capabilities, but Shotcut's editing options are there for you to try no matter what your experience level is.

Link Download https://www.shotcut.org/

3. VirtualDub2 Video Editor

VirtualDub2 (previously known as VirtualDub FilterMod) is based on the well-known VirtualDub open source application and it includes features from different projects: x264 encoder, lagarith encoder, fflayer filter, etc.

This collection of tools is portable, which means you don't have to install the application on your computer and have your Windows registry modified.

No traces are left when the software is removed and you can keep VirtualdubMod on your computer or on a memory device.

VirtualdubMod allows you to process videos the easy way, due to its intuitive, uncluttered interface. It offers all the features originally found in VirtualDub and it supports MPEG2 and AC3; it can also work with corrupt AC3 and MP3 files.

The output video can be easily extracted by specifying the start and the end points and you can apply various filters and effects: modifying brightness level, inverting colors, flipping, blurring, and many others.

VirtualdubMod has not been developed anymore for a long time, so it was replaced by VirtualDub2.

Link Download *https://sourceforge.net/projects/vdfiltermod/*

4. AviSynth Video Editor

AviSynth is a software tool for video post-production which uses specialized scripts and no graphical interface. Once you master it, you can apply unrestricted and extensive editing options to your video files.

This application is designed rather for professionals, but AviSynth is not such a restrictive tool if you study the documentation and learn its code lines.

Start with simple commands and after gaining experience, pass to more complex scripts. Scripts can be written in any simple text editor and saved as *.avs files. These files can be opened afterwards by using a media player.

Although AviSynth can process a wide variety of video and audio files, it depends on the codecs you have previously installed on your PC. Editing can be performed, though, without needing temporary files, which ensures a higher speed. AviSynth enjoys support from other programs, as well, such as VirtualDubMod, StaxRip or AVSGenie. These applications allow you to create scripts and to apply various filters and effects.

With AviSynth, when you load the script into a compatible media player (Windows Media Player, Light Alloy, Gom Player, etc), you don't have to add any extra input. The script is read like any other video and you'll soon enjoy the complex series of effects you have applied.

Even if the need to learn new commands may discourage some users in the beginning, AviSynth is definitely a better choice, especially for professionals which need to process a large amount of video files. The result is much faster with this piece of software than it would be by using applications which feature a GUI.

AviSynth's complexity is only exceeded by its power. This application is definitely the best choice if you want to process videos like an expert, in ways you would not have imagined before.

Link Download *https://sourceforge.net/projects/avisynth2/*

5. VSDC Free Video Editor

VSDC Free Video Editor does exactly what its name suggests: it enables you to add effects to your videos and change various parameters without needing to spend money on expensive software.

Furthermore, you can convert videos to your format of choice using intuitive commands.

You can create videos at various complexity levels, and both novices and experienced computer users will find this piece of software handy.

The program's simple interface is backed by rich functions that allow you to create the exact video you have in mind.

VSDC Free Video Editor is a non-linear editing tool, which means that objects can be placed in any position on the video timeline, regardless of their size. Their shape, parameters and position can change arbitrarily over time.

It's important to know that VSDC Free Video Editor supports the most common formats (audio, video and image); there is no need for extra tools to edit your files. Moreover, you can create videos for popular devices like smartphones, PSP, Xbox, Archos, Zune, iRiver, Blackberry, Creative Zen, and many others.

The video effects you can apply to VSDC Free Video Editor are extremely numerous, and they were divided into 5 categories, helping users to identity the effect they need more easily: color correction, object transformation, transition effects, object filters, and special fix.

VSDC Free Video Editor is easy to use, but more complex than other similar free apps. Besides converting between the most popular file formats, applying effects, and creating videos for various devices, VSDC Free Video Editor includes other features as well, such as working with charts, an upcoming video library, DVD burning, video download manager, desktop video capture, and video capturing.

The wide range of features provided by VSDC Free Video Editor allows you to obtain professional videos with minimum effort.

Link Download http://www.videosoftdev.com/free-video-editor

6. Vidiot Video Editor

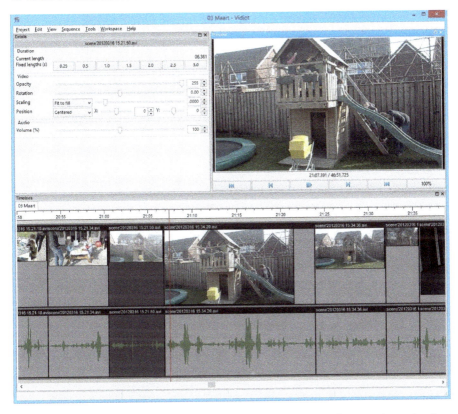

Vidiot helps you edit videos and perform operations such as scaling, rotating, trimming, compositing, adding transitions, and so on. The video formats supported by this non-linear video editor include AVI, MOV and MP4. Vidiot also provides support for GIFs and JPGs and for sound files such as WAV and MP3.

After a fast and straightforward installation process, you will have access to Vidiot's simple layout.

Less experienced users may feel disorientated in the beginning, but soon enough you should be able to discover the main features.

A comprehensive help file is available for beginners. Once you get used to it, this piece of software makes your work easier and helps you save time by loading the last project at startup and creating backups of saved files when overwriting them.

Your videos can be previewed in Vidiot's built-in media player and you will be able to instantly make an idea on how the final clip will look like.

Some editing options provided by Vidiot include adjusting volume level, changing video opacity, scaling the clip, rotating images to various angles, removing empty tracks, splitting videos, and inserting fade in and out effects between clips. Audio and video streams can be viewed separately for editing.

Vidiot delivers good performance by using a low amount of computer resources and is extremely easy to use. The app includes drag and drop support, allowing you to import files in a convenient manner. What you'll appreciate the most about Vidiot will be the good quality of exported files. However, Vidiot doesn't do everything you'd expect from a video editor; for instance, it is not able to slow down or speed up clips.

In spite of its limited features and basic design, Vidiot can do a great job if you want to perform some common editing tasks and will deliver very good performance on any computer.

Link Download *https://sourceforge.net/projects/vidiot/*

7. VideoPad Video Editor

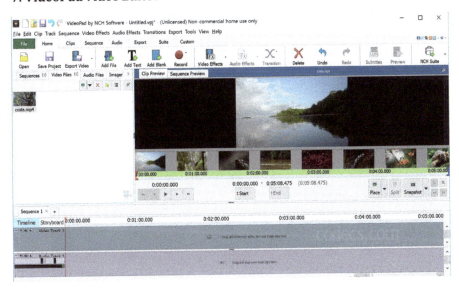

VideoPad is an easy-to-use editing software for creating professionally-looking videos. Editing your videos will be a child's play and you'll be able to put all your ideas into practice due to the various tools provided by this application.

As you open the main window, you will notice that the features of this program are well-organized under the following sections: Media List, Transitions, Effects, Clips, Files, Video Track, Audio Track, Overlay Track and so on.

You can use input from a camcorder, a webcam of TV card, too. Just drag and drop videos and start playing with them.

VideoPad Video Editor supports the most common video formats, including WMV, AVI, WMV, 3GP, DIVX, XVID, MPEG, MP4, MOV, VOBB, OGM, H.264 etc. You can also use images and audio elements, such as BMP, JPG, JPEG, GIF, PSD, TIFF, TGA, respectively MP3, WAV, M4A, MPGA, MID, AAC, FLAC, WMA, OGG, VOX, CDA and many others.

Apart from adding various elements to your videos, you can also set overlays and blank sides, change playback speed, apply audio and video effects, record your voice over the video, apply transitions and so on.

The output is extremely versatile. Once you have finished your editing session and are satisfied with the results, you can burn the video on a DVD, CD or Blu-ray to play it on TV, export it to a mobile device (iPod, iPhone, PSP etc.) or share it on YouTube, directly from the VideoPad window.

All things considered, VideoPad Video Editor is an application worth trying; it offers a variety of editing tools, it allows you to share the resulting videos online or burn them on a disk, it has a good overall performance and it needs a medium amount of system resources to function.

Link Download https://www.nchsoftware.com/videopad/

8. Windows Live Movie Maker

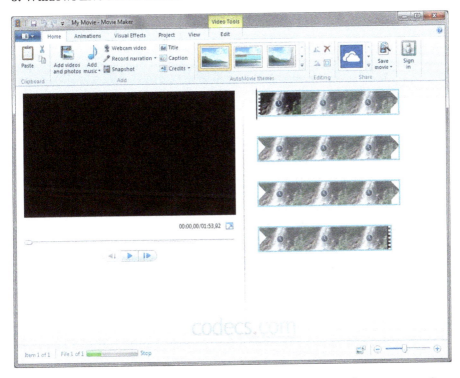

Windows Live Movie Maker is a video editing tool from Windows which allows you to transform your photos and videos in amazing movies.

This utility has a lot of editing tools to offer you and it also allows you to easily share the results with your friends.

One of the strengths of Windows Live Movie Maker is the fact it accepts various types of media (videos and photos).

All these contents from your computer are nicely organized within a Windows Live Photo gallery so they are always ready to hand.

Windows Live Movie Maker allows you to obtain the perfect blend between sound and images, and it puts at your disposal a variety of tools: themes, transitions, visual effects, text for title, captions and credits, fade effects, speed adjusting, split and trim options. Use transitions as much as you wish in order to obtain a professional-looking video.

After finishing the job, just post the video on the Internet, directly from Windows Live Movie Maker. You can share it to YouTube, Facebook, Windows Live SkyDrive and many others.

You can also send the output to mobile devices or you can burn it on DVD discs. In the second case, you need to have Windows DVD Maker installed on your computer. This utility is available if you have installed on your computer one of the following operating systems: Windows 7 Home Premium, Windows 7 Professional, Windows 7 Enterprise, Windows 7 Ultimate, Windows Vista Home Premium, and Windows Vista Ultimate editions.

Thanks to Windows Live Movie Maker, it is not difficult to get your own home videos and make them look professional.

From importing media contents that you will use to create your video to sharing the result online, Windows Live Movie Maker is there for you at every step.

Link Download *http://www.free-codecs.com/windows_live_movie_maker_download.htm*

9. Gsplit Video Editor

Gsplit comes in handy when you need to split large files into smaller pieces. Let's say you want to send a large file such as a compressed archive via email, but its size exceeds the limit set by your email provider.

In this case Gsplit allows you to divide the large file into a set of smaller files called pieces.

Other uses of Gsplit besides making it easier to send large files by email are preparing files for storage devices, copying data to CD and DVD, uploading files to online file hosting sites that have file size restrictions, and sending files on Instant Messenger apps.

Very large files, even bigger than 4 GB, are supported without any trouble.

Gsplit is suitable for all types of users, from novice ones to advanced. Files can only be imported by using the file browser, but on the other hand, batch processing is enabled in order to ease your work.

There are two types of splitting supported by Gsplit – by size or by number of parts. You can either enter the size of each resulting file or require a certain number of pieces. During the splitting operation the elapsed and estimated times are being displayed.

Next you can customize piece files and change their name, title, author, and other properties. You can create pieces without tags or with custom headers, in case you are working with CSV files.

Gsplit also allows the opposite operation, joining files back together. The app creates an executable file enabling you to put cut pieces back together, without launching Gsplit again.

Don't worry about the risk of obtaining corrupt files; Gsplit is able to perform fast checks and detect file corruption.

Gsplit is highly recommended to any Windows user – the program uses a reasonable amount of resources, completes operations fast, and runs error-free.

Link Download *http://www.gdgsoft.com/gsplit/index.aspx*

10. SolveigMM AVI Trimmer Video Editor

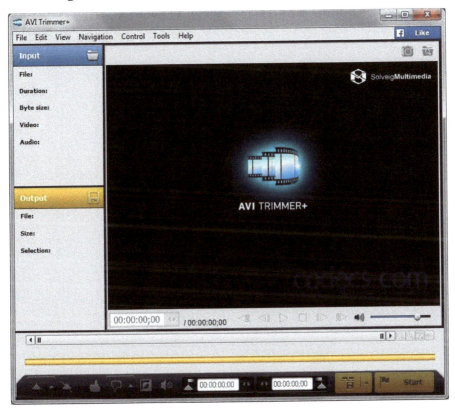

SolveigMM AVI Trimmer + is a powerful application which allows you to cut pieces from AVI and MKV videos without needing to encode or decode video files. By using this trimmer, you will avoid video and audio degradation and synchronization problems after editing.

The AVI Trimmer + supports, as its name suggests, both AVI and MKV files.

Moreover, the application also supports AVI and MKV files embedding other types of video and audio content.

To be more precise, the file formats supported by AVI Trimmer + are AVI type 1 and 2; OpenDML AVI; AVI files with any video content such as DivX, XviD, MPEG4 and so on; AVI files with different audio contents, including AC3, OGG and MPEG 1,2 Layer I, II, III; AVI files with VBE

MPEG audio; AVI files exceeding 4 GB; MKV format files and MKV files with various types of video content: AVC, MPEG4, DivX, XviD and with any audio content.

Other features of the AVI Trimmer + you should know about are the following: it's based on the Solveig Video Editing Engine; it allows trimming AVI files containing VBR audio without synchronization loss; it can cut various portions of a movie at one time so you can eliminate unwanted commercials and it supports the OpenDML AVI file format extension.

AVI and MKV files can be imported only by using the file browser; the "drag and drop" method is not supported. Fragments you want to cut can be easily selected by marking the starting and the ending point.

An up-to-date tool, AVI Trimmer + is strongly recommended to anyone who wants to easily cut multiple video file fragments. No matter what type of AVI or MKV file you want to process, this application will do the job.

Link Download *http://www.free-codecs.com/avi_trimmer_download.htm*

11. MPEG4 Modifier Video Editor

MPEG4 Modifier is an editing tool which enables you to modify MPEG4 videos (XviD and DivX) without re-encoding. Avoiding re-encoding saves time and resources, and this is the main advantage of MPEG4 Modifier, compared to other editors.

The actions you can perform in MPEG4 Modifier are changing aspect ratio, editing user data, removing or adding packed bitstream, changing interlaced field order, finding out information about the video, such as the amount of I/P/S/B-VOPs used, if QPel/GMC were used or not and so on. Nevertheless, the movie must be found in an AVI container.

A thing you need to be aware of is that aspect ratio modification works by changing a flag in the VOL headers, which is ignored by most decoders.

To sum up, MPEG4 Modifier is easy to use and reliable; it needs a very low amount of resources and it helps you save time by not using any conversion methods.

Link download http://moitah.net/

12. VidePub Video Editor

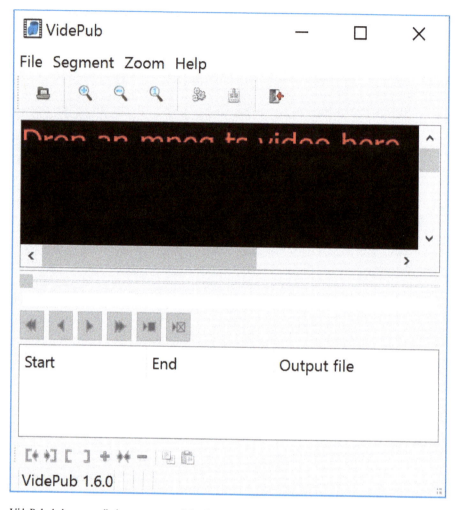

VidePub helps you eliminate commercials from TV recordings fast and easy. The video formats supported by this application are MPEG-2 TS and H.264 TS. The method used by VidePub is eliminating sequences which do not contain the channel logo.

TV channels usually display their logo during programs or films, and remove it when they broadcast commercials.

By eliminating video portions without the logo, you should enjoy a commercial-free recording.

Aside from the automatic commercial removal feature, you can also select desired sequences manually and choose the exact portions you want to remove.

The input format is preserved, as no re-encoding process is performed, which makes VidePub fast and easy to use.

The VidePub pack contains the installer, a ReadMe file, and a user manual. There is also a French version of the user manual.

VidePub runs on Windows XP, Vista, 7, 8 and 10.

VidePub is a smart tool enabling you to remove TV commercials with very little effort, in case commercial sequences lack the channel logo, and also to manually specify the portions you want to eliminate. Due to its straightforward interface and user manual, this utility is recommended to all categories of users.

Link Download *http://www.arthelion.com/index.php/en/*

15. Openshot Video Editor

OpenShot Video Editor is a free and open-source video editor for FreeBSD, Linux, macOS, and Windows. The project was started in August 2008 by Jonathan Thomas, with the objective of providing a stable, free, and friendly to use video editor.

OpenShot's core video editing functionality is implemented in a C++ library, libopenshot. OpenShot uses the Qt toolkit and offers a Python API.

OpenShot supports commonly used codecs that are supported by FFmpeg, including WebM (VP9), AVCHD (libx264), HEVC (libx265), and audio codecs such as mp3 (libmp3lame) and aac (libfaac). The program can render MPEG4, ogv, Blu-ray, and DVD video, and Full HD videos for uploading to Internet video web sites.

Link Download *http://www.openshot.org/*

www.ingramcontent.com/pod-product-compliance
Lightning Source LLC
Chambersburg PA
CBHW041635050326
40689CB00024B/4972